SUZHOU
A Garden City

SUZHOU
A Garden City

FOREIGN LANGUAGES PRESS   BEIJING

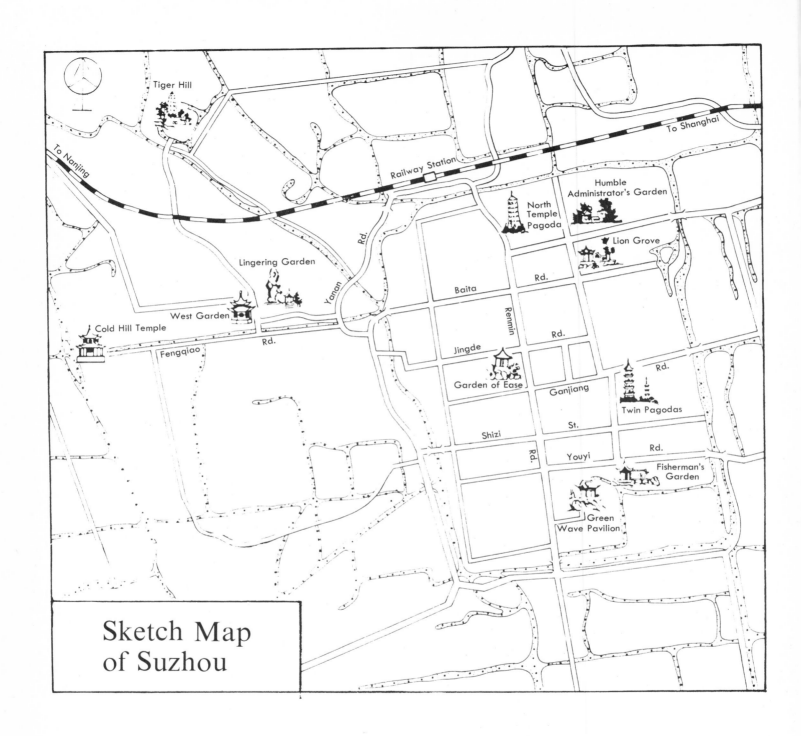

Sketch Map of Suzhou

Tiger Hill

To Nanjing

To Shanghai

Railway Station

North Temple Pagoda

Humble Administrator's Garden

Lion Grove

Lingering Garden

Yanan Rd.

Baita

Rd.

Renmin

West Garden

Cold Hill Temple

Fengqiao

Rd.

Jingde

Rd.

Garden of Ease

Ganjiang

Twin Pagodas

St.

Shizi

Rd.

Youyi

Rd.

Fisherman's Garden

Green Wave Pavilion

Contents

Suzhou Gardens
— Architectural Masterpieces

Suzhou in Jiangsu Province is a city of beauty. Its traditional-style gardens, in particular, have been appreciated through the centuries by Chinese and world travelers as architectural masterpieces. They do in fact harmonize natural, painted and poetic beauty, give fine expression to the art of architecture, and are treasures among China's cultural legacies.

Landscape gardening in China dates back to the Yin (also known as Shang) and Zhou dynasties more than 3,000 years ago when "enclosures" planted to trees and stocked with fowl and animals served the monarchs as hunting grounds. In the Qin (221-207 B.C.) and Han (206 B.C.-A.D. 220) dynasties there were built in these "enclosures" magnificent hunting lodges for monarchs on their tours out of the capital. In time, lesser imperial families and noble households followed suit, building gardens of their own, though pared down in scale. Imitating nature, they cultivated flowers, had trees planted, ponds dug and the earth piled up in artificial hills. As more ponds were dug, the mounds increased, until the gardens were practically either hills or water. In the Tang (618-907) and Song (960-1279) dynasties these "hill and water" gardens multiplied. Scholars, officials, wealthy merchants and landowners began building gardens around or near their dwellings, a degree of popularization that led to notable improvement in the art of garden architecture and a flourishing of rustic charm in great variety. Suzhou gardens were laid out from the 10th to the 19th century, throughout the Song, Yuan (1271-1368), Ming (1368-1644) and Qing (1644-1911) dynasties. The Green Wave Pavilion (*Cang Lang Ting*), Lion Grove (*Shi Zi Lin*), Humble Administrator's Garden (*Zhuo Zheng Yuan*),

Lingering Garden (*Liu Yuan*), West Garden (*Xi Yuan*), Fisherman's Garden (*Wang Shi Yuan*) and Garden of Ease (*Yi Yuan*) represent respectively the artistic style of those four dynasties.

Records of Suzhou place the number of gardens built there during the Ming and Qing dynasties at two hundred. Why was there this great concentration of gardens at Suzhou?

Favourably situated in the mild climate south of the Changjiang (Yangtze) River, Suzhou has the added attraction of the nearby Taihu Lake. Poets and artists gathered here over the 24 centuries of the city's history. Because of its natural beauty and economic prosperity it became a fashionable place for officials, rich merchants and landlords who bought land there and engaged artisans, poets, painters and landscape gardeners to create gardens in the gentle atmosphere of which they could prolong their lives and make them as pleasant as possible.

Suzhou gardens differ from China's imperial gardens, which usually covered large scenic areas outside the city and were filled in with palace-style structure while improving in general on natural features and then landscaping the whole. Magnificently symmetrical, built on elevations to impress the common people with the transcending power of the throne, they were designed to strike fear and awe into the hearts of the populace.

Suzhou gardens on the other hand were invariably privately owned household gardens, each a single unit secluded within high walls in the residential area of the city proper. Small in scale, Suzhou gardens are miniature scenes duplicated from nature. Halls, pavilions and terraces are meticulously and elegantly constructed, then set in a manner that is convincingly natural.

The structuring of a Suzhou garden begins with the careful choice of location. Next comes the placing of the main hills, ponds and buildings according to the geographical features and size of the area. Ornamental rocks are then placed, and trees and shrubs planted. Accessory structures are added so as to achieve an organic whole, while the arrangement of flowers and trees around the hills, ponds, springs, rocks, pavilions, terraces and halls is highly artistic. The idea is to enable the garden devotee to enjoy natural beauty without leaving the convenience and privacy of the high walls enclosing his property.

As with other Chinese gardens, those of Suzhou feature mainly buildings, hills, bodies of water, flowers and trees. Buildings focus on halls surrounded by pavilions, terraces and towers which, though independent, are connected by bridges, galleries with window patterns and moon-shaped gates. The whole garden appears as if in "layers" of roofs, rocks and water, yet with each component standing on its own. A Suzhou garden may be lived in as well as enjoyed esthetically.

Artificial hills are constructed of rocks, earth and special Taihu rocks, which are limestone quarried from the West Hill Island in the Taihu Lake. Masons in ancient times made rough carvings in selected pieces of limestone, chiseling into them or cutting out the desired designs, then submerging the rocks in the lake for years until they were eroded into strange shapes.

Ground water at Suzhou is found only two metres below the surface and ponds are readily dug.

Most are long and narrow. A main body of water is generally let into smaller ponds of various dimensions, miniature islands, bridges, dams and pavilions being used to divert its flow. An intricate water pattern and one or more small bends are favoured to produce the artistic effect of paths winding through hills and over or along water to lead one to a place shaded by willows and beautiful with flowers. The building of Suzhou gardens is guided by the principle of "elevating mounds with ornamental rocks and digging ponds in low-lying land" and that of "hills skirted by water and water embellishing hills".

Flowers, shrubs and trees are selected by skilled landscape gardeners from among the hundred-some choice garden plants and trees found in Suzhou. The watchword in arrangement is naturalness, to avoid uniformity, regularity and symmetry in the plantings. Inspiration is taken from poetry and painting describing charming landscapes. Flowers are displayed throughout the four seasons.

The following guidelines are generally followed in building Suzhou gardens:

Restraint. A sort of suspense is achieved by leading through twists and turns onto a breath-taking scene. This "restraint", or labyrinthine, often shaded entry into a grand, sunlit open space, is one of the fascinations of the gardens.

Artistic screening. Along the passageway to a grand view are encountered rocky hills or woods to allow no more than a glimpse into the inner garden before it comes into full view. The effect is one of constant change of scene as the garden stroller progresses. Old Chinese classics describe this device:

"As in writing poetry, garden building requires nuances as well as unity and balance. Encumbrances and overloading of the landscape with accessory structures and 'gingerbread' are, however, ruled out in order to attain good taste."

Framing. Doorways, gates and windows are used as ornamental frames for selected scenes. These are rectangular, square, round, vase-shaped or polygonal, with meticulously composed views of a rockery, a tree or grove, a pavilion or hall behind to be ornamentally framed by them.

Contrast. Density contrasting with sparseness of objects, depth versus breadth of space, precipitous rockeries set against sparkling water, exquisite buildings against natural flowers and trees, as well as contrasting colours, textures and forms are all utilized.

Borrowing. This refers to utilizing the natural scenes or buildings outside the garden in a way that all are made into a harmonic whole and a sense of extended space and novelty lent to the garden.

Very important in displaying the separate garden scenes while giving them unity is their linking up by one or more interesting paths, called sightseeing routes. The routes are either galleries or other passageways around the hills and pools, or paths leading up the hills and across the waters via tiny bridges. The sightseeing routes are circular or criss-crossing so that scenes in the garden are viewed from different angles.

In short, a great variety of artistic methods are used in Suzhou gardens to produce in miniature a true representation of nature. It is remarkable that such quiet gardens existed amid the noise and bustle of old Suzhou.

Skilled gardeners are legion in Suzhou's history, and some gardening specialists were particularly renowned for their art. Zhu Mian, born in Suzhou during the Northern Song Dynasty (960-1127) into a family of garden architects for several generations, was known as "Gardener Zhu". The Zhu family left their definite mark on garden building in Suzhou. Ji Cheng, born in 1573 during the Ming Dynasty, was a master painter who collected odd and interesting rocks and became distinguished for his artistry in garden building. Officials called him into service, and he left for posterity no few celebrated gardens. Further, he recorded his theoretical and practical experience in *On Garden-building Art* in three volumes. Ji Cheng's influence is seen especially in the arrangement of views and making of artificial hills in Suzhou gardens.

Chinese garden-building art emphasizes natural beauty. Though man-made, a Chinese garden does not appear artificial, but as a spot of nature in miniature. This is different from the geometric, regular and grand style of gardens in the West.

Japan adopted the Chinese gardening style first, with Buddhism and its requirement of quiet meditation introduced there from China in the sixth century. Ji Cheng's *On Garden-building Art* was hand-copied in Japan.

The Chinese influence on European garden-building art dates from the 18th century as evidenced by the remains of no less than 20 gardens built in Chinese style found in one district of Paris.

The North Temple Pagoda (*Bei Si Ta*), a typical Buddhist tower of brick and wood in the city proper, was built 1,400 years ago. A spiral staircase takes the energetic visitor to the top storey.

Suzhou: An Ancient City

Suzhou is located about 100 kilometres west of Shanghai, about an hour and a half by train. The landmark that first strikes the visitor's eye on arrival is the imposing North Temple Pagoda (*Bei Si Ta*).

The pagoda as it was first built between 502 and 556 had 11 storeys, but civil strife took its toll in subsequent years, and it was rebuilt in 1162 as a nine-storey, wood-and-brick Buddhist tower. The pagoda is now one of the city's major historic buildings and is under state protection.

Suzhou has many such historic and unique structures. Among the others are the Twin Pagodas (*Shuang Ta*) and the Auspicious Light Pagoda (*Rui Guang Ta*), which also contribute to the architectural style and atmosphere of this ancient Chinese garden city.

A memorable feature of Suzhou is its rivers, canals and arched stone bridges. Sampans ply its streets of water, their oars creaking in rhythm.

A Tang Dynasty poet has left us the following lines:

Have you ever been in Suzhou
Where every house pillows on water?
Ancient palaces filled with pavilions,
Canals and bridges too many to count.
Buy caltrops and lotus root at a night market;
Silks and satins weigh down junks in spring. . . .

The Twin Pagodas (*Shuang Ta*) southeast of the city were built nearly 1,000 years ago.

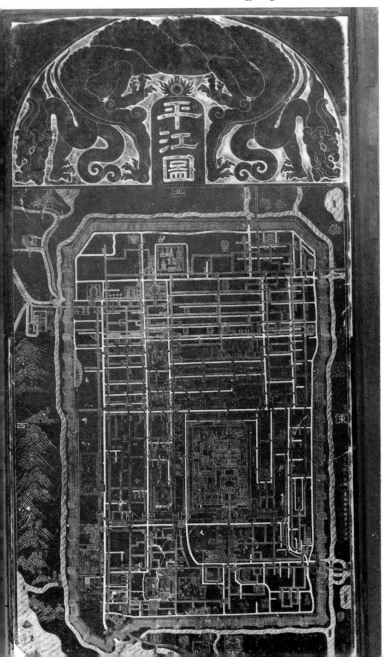

Stone map of Suzhou carved in the Song Dynasty (960-1279), when the city was known as Pingjiang Prefecture.

Suzhou was flourishing 1,000 years ago. The Song Dynasty city map carved in stone, which is now preserved in the Suzhou Museum, shows the area criss-crossed with six north-south and 14 east-west canals spanned by more than 350 bridges. The streets run parallel with the rivers or canals, which are lined with houses, the stoops at their back doors being places where water is drawn and laundry done. At evening boats would moor by the houses, while during the day they sailed by in a constant stream. One can still find such Song Dynasty scenes in Suzhou today.

Marco Polo, who visited Suzhou in 1275 during the Yuan Dynasty, travelled its every street and suburb, canal and lake, and wrote that Suzhou was as thriving and charming as Venice, his home city.

Favourably located geographically and climatically on the southwestern Changjiang (Yangtze) River delta, Suzhou is fertile and warm. Fifteen kilometres to its southwest is the Taihu, one of China's biggest freshwater lakes. Streams from it flow through Suzhou and empty into the Changjiang. East of the city stretches a plain patterned with a network of rivers and canals, connecting with lakes and ponds, the largest being the Yangcheng, Jinji and Huangtiandang lakes. These automatically regulate the volume of flow of the rivers, irrigate rice-paddy, and prevent flooding. Suzhou's economy continues to flourish with the cultivation of the multi-use lotus and caltrops, ducks, geese and fish, added to rich agricultural yields and the development of silk-weaving and embroidery. Water navigation is a boon. Boats carrying Suzhou brocade and embroidery sail unimpeded to the southeast seacoast and back to Suzhou laden with local merchandise. Suzhou has for centuries been an economic and trade hub of southeastern China.

Suzhou's history dates back more than 25 centuries. In the sixth century B.C., when many princely states were striving for supremacy in China, the State of Wu arose in the Taihu Lake area and grew powerful under King Zhu Fan who, in 560 B.C., made Suzhou his capital and had walls built around it. When He Lü succeeded to the throne in 515 B.C., the State of Wu was strong and prosperous enough for him to renovate and extend his capital

A waterside view of Hill River Bank Street (*San Tang Jie*) in Suzhou.

Sunset on one of the ten waterways in the city.

The city's many marble arched bridges give it a special charm.

The 1,500-year-old Grand Canal as it skirts the city to the west.

to a circumference of 23 kilometres, and to strengthen its enclosing wall and entrench it with moats. Confined by its waterways, Suzhou occupies essentially the same area as it did more than 2,000 years ago.

This flourishing situation nurtured the splendid culture of the lower Changjiang River centring around Suzhou. However, without the cultural infusion from the north which occurred in the Song Dynasty, Suzhou would not be the garden city as it is today.

In 1127 the Song capital was moved from Bianliang (present-day Kaifeng) to Lin'an (Hangzhou) after the north was repeatedly invaded and finally occupied by the Nüzhen Tartars, who inhabited China's northeastern border. The Song imperial family, high officials, nobles and scholars went south with the ancient and prestigious civilization and art of the Huanghe (Yellow) River valley in the central plain. Suzhou's natural attractions held this leisured class in Suzhou, and for many centuries the city with i

Entrance to the Cold Hill Temple (*Han Shan Si*).

wealth and gentility was a fashionable cultural and economic centre of southeast China.

Suzhou has produced outstanding artists and men of letters over the centuries. Ming Dynasty ink-and-colour landscape paintings of scenes around Suzhou are recognized to this day as unsurpassed masterpieces. Referred to as of the Wu School, these works greatly influenced the later Ming and the Qing dynasty paintings. They also inevitably influenced the construction of gardens, which are actually three-dimensional replicas of the landscape paintings but using rocks, ponds, pavilions, flowers and trees for paper, brush and pigment.

The delightful scenery and a mild climate that favoured prosperity, plus the cultural heritage from the north, were all conducive to building Suzhou into a "garden city".

The Grand Canal with a total length of 1,722 kilometres is the longest man-made waterway in the world. With terminals at Beijing and Hangzhou in Zhejiang Province, it was an important navigation channel linking China's north and south. Like the Great Wall, it represents tremendous engineering skill and muscle labour of ancient Chinese working people.

The digging began in 495 B.C. in western Suzhou as a military measure during the reign of King Fu Chai of the State of Wu and was continued section by section in succeeding dynasties. The first section of 150 kilometres extended north to the Huaihe River and cut through the Taihu Lake forming the first link between the Huaihe and the Changjiang river systems.

On the Grand Canal shore stands the Cold Hill Temple (*Han Shan Si*), mentioned by the Tang Dynasty poet Zhang Ji in his "Mooring at Night by Maple Bridge" and now often visited for its historic interest. Maple Bridge spans the Grand Canal here.

Sculptures of the monks Han Shan and Shi De in a side-room of the Arhat Hall at the Cold Hill Temple.

The Bell Tower and winding cloister at the Cold Hill Temple.

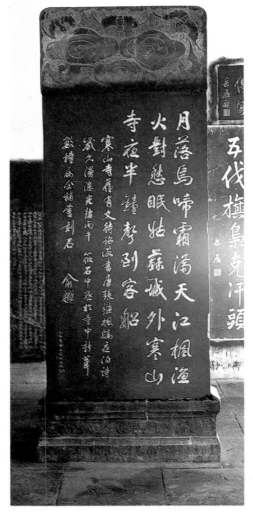

Exhibited in the temple's Tablet Room is a collection of inscriptions carved in stone. The nearest one bears the famous poem "Mooring at Night by Maple Bridge" by the Tang Dynasty poet Zhang Ji.

"First Tower by the Maple River" reads the plaque (*top left*). This tower at the temple affords panoramic views.

Pavilion amid autumn maples at the foot of the Sky Level Hill (*Tian Ping Shan*) about ten kilometres west of the city.

The Tiger Hill Pagoda on the Tiger Hill (*Hu Qiu Shan*) in autumn. The Tiger Hill, just outside the old city, is the most famous of Suzhou's sights.

The Cold Hill Temple was first built in the 17 years between 502 and 519. A venerable monk called Han Shan of the Tang Dynasty, together with another venerable monk, Shi De, are said to have lived in the temple. Hence its present name. The Maple Bridge in front of the temple became a busy market place, with boats mooring there on journeys on the Grand Canal. Here is Zhang Ji's poem:

> *The moon sets, a lone crow caws across the frosty sky*
> *As the fishing-boats' lights flicker sadly under the Maple Bridge.*
> *Beyond the city the bell of Cold Hill Temple*
> *Chimes for the coming of a passenger boat at midnight.*

Suzhou is a city with clear rivers and lakes in the eastern part and scenic hills to the west. The Miraculous Rock Hill (*Ling Yan Shan*) is one of these, while the Sky Level Hill (*Tian Ping Shan*) and the Tiger Hill (*Hu Qiu Shan*) also offer sites of historic interest. Of these, the Tiger Hill is known as "the foremost spot of historic interest in Suzhou".

Originally named Hill that Rose Out of the Sea (*Hai Yong Shan*), the Tiger Hill is three kilometres from the Suzhou city limits. Only 29 metres above sea level, it is more than 20 hectares in area. It was formerly the mausoleum of King He Lü who died in a war with the State of Yue in the south and was ceremoniously buried on the hill by his son Fu Chai. Three days after the funeral a white tiger is said to have crouched on the hill, giving it its present name.

This hill has captured the imagination since ancient times and

The White Water-Lily Pond and Nodding Rock on the Tiger Hill. The rock is said to have nodded in agreement and water-lilies to have sprung up in the pond when the monk Zhu Daosheng of the Jin Dynasty (265-420) declared: "Lay down your butcher's knife and you can become a Buddha on the spot," while expounding Buddhist doctrine here.

King He Lü's Sword-Testing Rock on the Tiger Hill.

The Thousand Persons Rock. When word got round that the Monk Zhu Daosheng could convince even a rock, over one thousand people gathered here to hear him. The inscriptions "Tiger Hill, Sword Pond" beside the moon gate were attributed to a Tang Dynasty calligrapher. Scholars later identified the two characters (Tiger Hill) on the right as having been done in a subsequent dynasty, hence the saying: "Fake Tiger Hill; genuine Sword Pond."

every stone, pond and pavilion has its story. Midway on the path up the hill is the Sword-Testing Rock cleft in the middle and said to have been where King He Lü tried the sharpness of a pair of precious swords named *Ganjiang* and *Moxie*. This legend leads one to believe that the skill of the Wu people as foundrymen thousands of years ago was indeed high. When Qin Shi Huang (First Emperor of the Qin Dynasty) on a tour south heard that King He Lü had been buried with 3,000 fine swords as funerary objects, he tried excavating the tomb to get them but failed, as the tomb was so well designed and firmly built. The Sword Pond is said to be the result of the digging. Other legend-shrouded objects on the hill are the Thousand Persons Rock, Nodding Rock, White Water-Lily Pond, as well as a pagoda and monastery.

The hills to the west of Suzhou form a part of the city's gardens, for like the others they are embellished with man-made objects. Here, artificial and natural hills and waters set off each other artistically and give Suzhou its reputation as the garden city of China.

The Third Spring, named by the Tang Dynasty tea connoisseur Lu Yu, whose clear, cool water is good for brewing tea. The First Spring is Gu Lian Quan in Lushan Mountain, Jiangxi and the Second Spring is Hui Shan Quan in Wuxi, Jiangsu. There are halls and pavilions nearby.

A stone tablet carving of the Green Wave Pavilion dating from the Emperor Guang Xu's reign (1875-1908) during the Qing Dynasty.

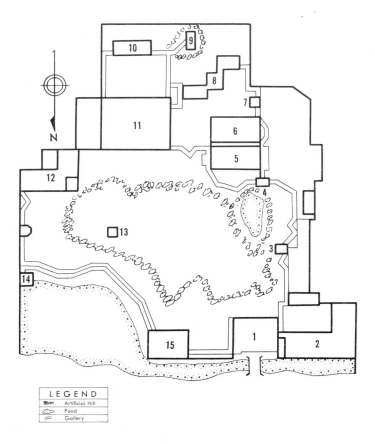

Green Wave Pavilion (*Cang Lang Ting*)

Situated inside Suzhou's South Gate, the Green Wave Pavilion is one of the city's celebrated gardens. It dates from the Song Dynasty, and having undergone reconstruction several times in the intervening seven centuries the garden's history throws light on the evolution of Suzhou garden-building art.

During the Five Dynasties (907-60) Suzhou was one of the cities ruled by Qian Liu, King of the State of Wuyue. Peace reigned in south China and prosperity followed, in contrast to the turmoil in the north. The rulers of Suzhou therefore began to indulge in building gardens and villas on a luxurious scale. Among these was the famous South Garden (*Nan Yuan*), of which the Green Wave Pavilion was part.

A man named Su Shunqin of the Song Dynasty bought the garden and had the pavilion built beside water, naming it Green Wave Pavilion, inspired by a favourite poem of that title. Su Shunqin himself wrote *Accounts of the Green Wave Pavilion*, which became popular. Ouyang Xiu (1007-72), a well-known poet of the time, and Su's other poet-friends, also praised the pavilion in verse, which added to its fame. The garden at that time consisted mainly of sizable hills and water areas, and exhibited a large variety of flowers set against bamboo. After Su Shunqin's death, the garden passed into the hands of several different owners and was reconstructed in a larger area. Later the Green Wave Pavilion was demolished in war and the garden premises were in bad repair.

During the reign of Emperor Kang Xi (1662-1722) of the Qing Dynasty, the provincial governor Song Luo had the pavilion rebuilt on top of a hill but gave it its original name as indicated by a plaque bearing the characters "Green Wave Pavilion" written by the great Ming Dynasty calligrapher-painter Wen Zhengming

In the morning mist and over the stone bridge lies the gate to the garden of Green Wave Pavilion.

(1470-1559). Song Luo also had a pavilion, the Self Mastery Tower (*Zi Sheng Xuan*), and another, the Fish-Viewing Pavilion (*Guan Yu Ting*), erected by a stream. He had a long crooked gallery built and named it Winding Walk (*Bu Qi*). But from that time on no major constructions were added.

After China's liberation in 1949 a renovation was undertaken aiming to restore the garden as it had been during the Qing Dynasty, and this incorporated features from the Song. The survival of the garden through long years of ill use and neglect is in itself remarkable. Its hills and ponds remained, weathering bitter winds and frosts through the ages to blossom out in China's spring.

The beautiful scenery outside the Green Wave Pavilion proper is given added charm by a stream flowing from west to east and past the garden gate on the north. In early summer lotus blossoms spread fragrance and a blaze of pink from their pools, while willow fronds reach to the water. The stream is banked with rockeries in a structural harmony that appears fascinatingly natural and ancient. The Fish-Viewing Pavilion, the Waterfront Pavilion (*Mian Shui Xuan*) and Lotus Fragrance Waterside Hall (*Ou Xiang Shui Xie*), as their names indicate, are all beside water. Rockeries and pavilions reflected in the water lend tranquility.

Hills mainly feature this garden. Passing the stone bridge before its gate one immediately sees an artificial hill composed of rocks and earth. Old trees supporting vines and ferns, along with bamboo, give an atmosphere of virgin forest in a mountain valley. The combining of earth with rocks to create artificial hills was a method used even before the Yuan Dynasty, when it was widely adopted to save manpower and materials and effect a natural-looking scene. Success in this skill was recognized only when an artificial hill could not be distinguished from a natural one. The earth provided nourishment for shrubs, their roots in turn binding earth and rocks together. Such a hill withstood erosion, while the shrubs complemented the rocks with their leaves and blossoms.

The Green Wave Pavilion is reached by following the winding pathway up the central hill. The original plaque with its inscription by Wen Zhengming is still over the doorway. The pillars of the pavilion are also inscribed with lines by the Song Dynasty poet Ouyang Xiu:

Fresh breeze and bright moon are treasures beyond price;
Water nearby and hills far off move one no end.

The garden buildings are set around the hill and connected by long galleries. The Bright Path Hall (*Ming Dao Tang*), the main building southeast of the hill, faces the three-room Realm of Jade Splendour (*Yao Hua Jing Jie*). Between these is a spacious courtyard surrounded by galleries that is agreeably cool in summer. Southwest of the hall is the Hill-Viewing Tower (*Kan Shan Lou*) from which the green hills are visible beyond the immediate compact garden scene. To the south is the Five Hundred Sages Shrine (*Wu Bai Ming Xian Ci*) with its rows of 500 images carved in inverse relief along three walls. Most are of celebrities of the past two thousand years.

On the gallery walls west are exquisite stone carvings called "Five Old Men" and "Seven Old Men of the Green Wave Pavilion".

The Green Wave Pavilion is outstanding for its "borrowed scenes". A partitioned gallery winds along the stream outside the north gate. Walking along the gallery, one has the feeling of strolling along a shady river bank. On the other side are more than 100 of latticed windows offering glimpses of scenery framed by their various shapes. Another characteristic of the garden is combining old and rigid styling along with the natural and graceful. Here, beauty resides in ingenuity and simplicity.

Morning and evening mists make the area in front of the garden's gate seem like an island.

This stream flows eastwards round the north side of the garden, then turns south to be like a moat around the garden, with overhanging willows and a stone embankment shoring it up. A partitioned gallery winds along the rocky bank. Latticed windows in the central wall can be looked through from either side, and this is known as "borrowing the scenery".

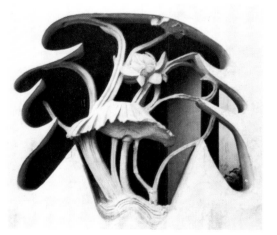

A sampling of the more than 100 ornamental windows in the Green Wave Pavilion garden.

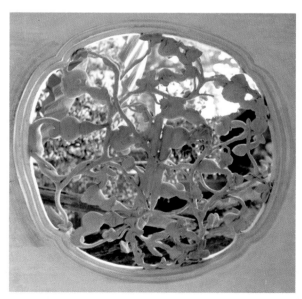

A vase-shaped gate.

The Green Wave Pavilion and partitioned gallery. The Green
Wave Pavilion, which gives the garden its name, on an artificial
hill that offers a view of the countryside southwest of Suzhou.

Gnarled wood furniture in the Bright Path Hall (*Ming Dao Tang*), the principal building of the garden.

This stone tablet done by masters' hands in ancient times is placed in the wall of a winding gallery. It bears a poem in praise of the "Seven Old Men of the Green Wave Pavilion" illustrated on it.

The water-carved rocks from the Taihu Lake are the most outstanding feature of the Lion Grove garden. This rockery is seen through a crabapple-blossom doorway.

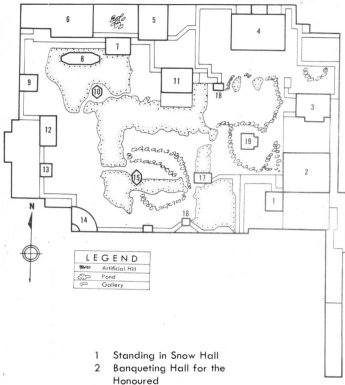

Lion Grove
(*Shi Zi Lin*)

During the reign of Emperor Zhi Zheng (1341-67) at the end of the Yuan Dynasty there came to Suzhou with his disciples a Buddhist monk of great repute named Tian Ru. This monk had a temple built on a Song Dynasty garden site (the present Garden Street of Suzhou) as a memorial to his teacher, the Buddhist monk Zhong Feng. And because the teacher had lived at the Lion Crag on the Tianmu Mountain outside Suzhou, the commemorative hall with its garden was named Lion Grove Temple (*Shi Lin Si*), or Lion Grove (*Shi Zi Lin*).

The renowned painter Ni Zan and others, together with a number of master garden architects, planned the construction. It consisted of a few simple buildings, its main feature being odd-shaped, steep rock hills, dense woods and bamboo groves. Later, the temple structures and garden came into private possession and a wall was built dividing the compound into two parts. The Buddha hall and the monastic rooms were in one part, while the garden formed the other. During the Qing Dynasty the emperors Kang Xi and Qian Long respectively visited the place while on inspection tours of south China. It is said that Emperor Qian Long mounted a hill in the northwestern part of the garden to view the scenery from the vantage point of a pavilion there. An able calligrapher, he put in brush writing on the spot: "Zhen you qu" ("It really fascinates"). An accompanying minister, feeling the expression too vulgar but unwilling to risk offending the emperor, diplomatically requested the gift from him of the middle word. This was done, and the more elegant "Zhen Qu" ("True Fascination") became the name of the pavilion. As the Qing emperor was a Lion Grove enthusiast, a replica was also built at

The Nestling-in-Clouds Pavilion (*Wo Yun Ting*) among the rocks of an artificial hill from which surrounding scenery may be viewed.

his Imperial Mountain Resort at Chengde in northern Hebei Province.

Still later this famous garden was purchased by a rich merchant named Bei who turned it over to the people's government upon the founding of the new China in 1949. It was opened to the public after renovation and repair.

The Lion Grove is small in area and nearly square in shape. Taihu rocks form the rockeries that are the main feature of its southeastern sector, while ponds characterize its northwest.

The Taihu rocks are fantastic in shape, some appearing like bamboo shoots, precipitous and towering above others. There are also huge rocks exquisitely carved out into concave and convex configurations by the action of the water in which they were submerged for years. Some are monstrously irregular; others appear as gentle but splendid cloud formations. From the top of the Cypress Tower (*Zhi Bai Xuan*) on the hill one sees initially

This "hill" in the southeast garden is a conglomerate of rocks carved into weird shapes by the action of water over centuries.

Rock formations stand like foothills to the main summit.

carved rocks suggesting lions in various postures — lying, prostrating, sitting on their haunches or standing on their hind legs with head tilted coyly to one side. Winding footpaths on the hill link stone caves of intriguing shapes. The stroller passes a Taihu rockery into the momentary darkness of a cave and then emerges suddenly into full daylight. The contour and exterior of each cave are different from the last.

Should one leave the proper path in favour of a shortcut, he will likely sense the frustration of finding himself back where he started after a short walk.

Another feature are good-sized trees growing out of crevices in artificial hills, providing canopies over them and bringing them to life.

Patterned in the main after odd-shaped Taihu rocks, the artificial hills of the Lion Grove are arranged according to the principle that "in landscape architecture, depth is the keynote and the essence of depth is twists and turns".

Rocks are used not only in building hills. They are also placed beside pools where they are reflected to produce an illusion of pools filled with these Taihu rocks. This, complementing the sector of the garden frankly composed of such bizarre rocks, makes the Lion Grove a small world of Taihu rocks.

The galleries in the Lion Grove wind up and down the low hills. One in the southeastern sector of the garden incorporates three pavilions, all built along walls which have sloping roofs over covered walkways on one side. These walls with built-in stone carvings and deep patterned windows do not appear to define the garden, an architectural method in Chinese landscape garden-building known as "combining the solid with the nebulous and vice versa".

Twisting footpaths, bridges and tunnels link stone carves in the hill. Each cave entrance frames a different scene.

The Mid-Lake Pavilion (*Hu Xin Ting*) in the northwest garden.

At the pool's southern tip the water is divided by rocks and a bridge.

The Taihu rocks in and around this pool lend depth and spaciousness to the scene.

Looking east across the garden.

Here water drips rhythmically from above.

The True Fascination Pavilion (*Zhen Qu Ting*) in the west garden from where it is said that the Qing emperors Kang Xi and Qian Long enjoyed the scenery.

A carved lantern and floral details of the natural hardwood in the ceiling. The wood carvings and ornaments in Suzhou gardens are usually unpainted.

Richly carved and ornamented arched ceiling of the Orchid Blossom Tower (*Hua Lan Lou*). The garden art of Suzhou combines architectural beauty with hill-and-water landscaping.

A floor-to-ceiling openwork screen of hardwood.

A carved hardwood balustrade.

A carved hardwood filigree
of delightful perfection
overhanging a doorway.

Humble Administrator's Garden
(*Zhuo Zheng Yuan*)

This garden dates back to the Ming Dynasty, some 400 years ago, and is done in the Ming style. Like other Suzhou gardens, it is mainly hills and water, in this instance treated so artistically as to make it a worthy representative of south China's ancient gardens.

The garden was opened to the public for the first time in 1954 after renovation as the Humble Administrator's Garden (*Zhuo Zheng Yuan*), its original name. Care was taken to preserve the artistic style of the Ming Dynasty — simplicity, elegance and serene.

"Quiet midst urban clamour", "enjoyment of mountain beauty without stepping outside the city", and "an unrestrained, leisurely happy and carefree life" were the watchwords in building the Humble Administrator's Garden.

In about the year 1513 Wang Xianchen, a court examiner of the

A lacquer carving showing the Humble Administrator's Garden.

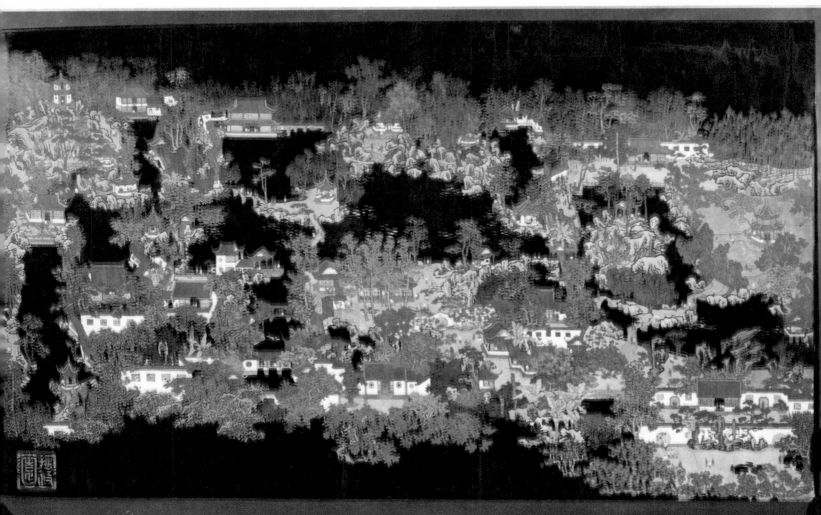

These views of the Humble Administrator's Garden are the works of the famous Ming Dynasty painter and calligrapher Wen Zhengming. They are preserved in the garden.

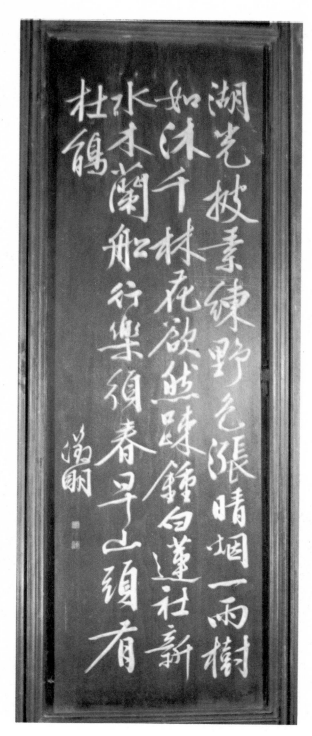

Verses by Wen Zhengming in his own calligraphy, inscribed on hardwood panels in one of the garden halls.

Ming Dynasty who lost court favour, settled in Suzhou. He had the garden built at the site of the Grand Temple (*Da Hong Si*). About 12 centuries earlier, an unsuccessful Jin Dynasty (265-420) official named Pan Yue had also returned to the soil as a gentleman farmer, planting trees and growing vegetables. It was Pan Yue who had penned the line "This is also the career of a humble administrator," which so much later gave the garden its name.

The Humble Administrator's Garden is the largest of Suzhou's old gardens, covering four hectares. Water is its chief feature, with ponds occupying three-fifths of the garden area. It is a copy of a small island named Water Reed Hill Island (*Lu Ding Shan Dao*) in the Taihu Lake.

1 Pavilion of Praiseworthy Honesty
2 Listening to Rain Hall.
3 Exquisite Hall
4 North Hill Pavilion
5 Crabapple Spring Hall
6 Silk Embroidery Pavilion
7 Parasol and Bamboo Hermitage
8 Green Ripple Pavilion
9 Fragrance of Snow and Cloud Pavilion
10 Lotus-Surrounded Pavilion
11 Hill-Viewing Tower
12 Pavilion of Reflections
13 Green Floating Pavilion
14 Lingering to Listen Pavilion
15 Thirty-Six Pairs of Mandarin Ducks Hall
16 Bamboo Hat Pavilion
17 Fan Pavilion
18 Pavilion of Double Delight
19 Pagoda Shaded Pavilion
20 Pine Wind Pavilion
21 Fragrance Isle (Moored Boat)
22 South Hall
23 Distant Fragrance Hall

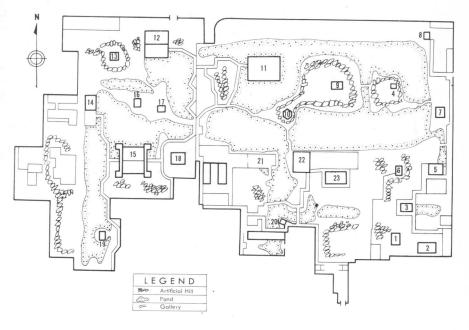

LEGEND
Artificial Hill
Pond
Gallery

Wisteria planted by Wen Zhengming, as the stone tablet records, still blossoms in a small courtyard west of the garden gate.

The east, central and west compounds of the Humble Administrator's Garden were at one time separate. The long-neglected east part, named Back to the Fields Garden (*Gui Tian Yuan*), was finally in 1955 equipped with a gate, teahouse and other buildings, and joined with the central and west compounds to form an integral whole. Studded with hills, pools, pavilions and halls in addition to terraces and green areas, the eastern part appears fresh and magnificent.

The central part of the Humble Administrator's Garden, about one hectare in area, is its gem. Entering the garden from the original gate, one comes first to a long and narrow lane leading to an inner gate, which opens onto an artificial hill obstructing the entire view of the garden's interior. The gallery west leads suddenly onto the panorama of the garden's main scenic area. The Distant Fragrance Hall (*Yuan Xiang Tang*), its chief attraction, is set against an artificial hill with a pool between. This device in garden arrangement is known as "concealing a scene before presenting it" and "contrasting spaces according to size".

The Distant Fragrance Hall was built during the Ming Dynasty. There are no pillars inside the hall to obstruct the view, but rather symmetrical latticed glass windows give onto all four sides, artistically framing certain scenes. The interior of the hall is decorated with potted plants through all four seasons, while a lotus pond graces it outside. In summer the fragrance of bright flowers among green leaves pervades the hall, giving it its name.

Terraces and ponds flank the north and south sides of the hall, with artificial hills. The southern hills are built tier upon tier of "layered" greenery, while the northern part dominates the landscape. The pond to the north is given an added impression of size by the East Hill Island and West Hill Island. These are linked to all appearances with greenery and rocks. Trees, flowering plants, bamboo, shrubs and vines on the islands and their banks all appear very natural.

The Awaiting Frost Pavilion (*Dai Shuang Ting*) and Fragrance of Snow and Cloud Pavilion (*Xue Xiang Yun Wei Ting*) are built on the two islands. The Fragrance of Snow and Cloud Pavilion has on its wall the lines by a Tang poet:

> *The shrill of cicadas enhances the tranquility of the garden;*
> *Bird songs set off the serenity of the hills.*

West of the Distant Fragrance Hall is a stone bridge called Little Flying Rainbow (*Xiao Fei Hong*), the only covered bridge in all the Suzhou gardens. It is slightly "camel-backed" with the roof supported by vermilion pillars. The name derives from its reflection in the moving water, an effect that is charming and novel. South of the Little Flying Rainbow stand three halls, while to its east and west are a pavilion and a gallery that form a courtyard of water. This quiet nook is called Miniature Green Wave Pavilion (*Xiao Cang Lang*), where water areas branch off to form a typically rustic scene of bends and inlets.

North of the Miniature Green Wave Pavilion is a building shaped like a pleasure boat. The fore part of this Moored Boat (*Han Chuan*) is surrounded by water on three sides, while the "stern" rests on the bank.

North of this are the Hill-Viewing Tower (*Jian Shan Lou*) and Lotus-Surrounded Pavilion (*He Feng Si Mian Ting*). The former is a vantage point from which one can gain a good view of the main scenic spots of the garden: the Little Flying Rainbow, Moored Boat, and pavilions and halls. The latter, the Lotus-Surrounded Pavilion, with its upswept eaves is also favourably located, its architectural style in complete harmony with the lotus ponds all around.

The buildings of the Humble Administrator's Garden are functional as well as ornamental. Halls were suited to entertaining

A pond in the central garden seen through a gallery window.

Ornamental window in the gallery wall.

his winding gallery sep-
rates the central and east-
rn parts of the garden.

This area in the east garden was renovated in 1955. The pond was dredged, the footbridges built, and trees and shrubs were planted. The Hibiscus Pavilion (*Fu Rong Xie*) offers good views of the east garden and is a pleasant place to sit.

With fewer buildings, the east garden gives the feel of the countryside.

The scene south of the Distant Fragrance Hall (*Yuan Xiang Tang*), the main hall in the central garden.

guests, towers and pavilions for seeing afar; studios provided the leisurely atmosphere for reading, chambers and lounges for rest. They were simple in construction and harmonized with nature. Buildings generally overlook water, galleries and terrace towers project from water. Though for the purpose of sightseeing, they take water as theme.

East of the Distant Fragrance Hall are sloped terraces planted to peonies. Beyond these lies a small loquat garden surrounded by undulating white cloud walls. An artificial hill here, crowned with a hall and two pavilions, is planted to loquat trees. The poetic line "picking loquats from a gold-laden tree" inspired an arrangement that gives the illusion of the fruit trees being within easy reach of visitors at loquat-picking time.

The arrangement of plants is the main feature of the Humble Administrator's Garden. During the Ming Dynasty there were 31 points of interest, of which 19 centre on plants, whether lotus,

Architectural elegance within the Distant Fragrance Hall.

Potted plants are on display throughout the year in the Distant Fragrance Hall.

A lotus pond north of the hall from which in early summer comes the fragrance of lotus, while the pond is a blaze of pink colour.

North of the Distant Fragrance Hall is the garden's main view, with the city's North Temple Pagoda in the background.

hibiscus, bamboo, willow, pine, rose bushes and vines, or such fruit trees as tangerine, loquat, peach, plantain, plum and crabapple. The Distant Fragrance Hall features lotus; the Loquat Garden, loquat trees; the Awaiting Frost Pavilion, tangerines; the Fragrance of Snow and Cloud Pavilion, plum.

In the late Qing Dynasty the western part of the Humble Administrator's Garden was walled off by a big landlord named Zhang Luqian, who took possession and named it "Zhang Garden Annex". His reconstruction was less natural than the original, though it remained basically the same.

A hall with a square room at each of its four corners has a crooked pond on its north and east sides, the hall itself being divided in the middle. The rear of the hall is named Thirty-Six Pairs of Mandarin Ducks Hall (*San Shi Liu Yuan Yang Guan*) from the fact that this number of ducks were once kept in the water north of the hall. A choice variety called "Camellia Eighteen",

once grown in the yard of the hall, lends its name to the front section (*Shi Ba Man Tuo Luo Hua Guan*). This hall was the site of entertaining guests at banquets and Kunqu Opera. Servants waited in the square rooms at their masters' beck and call, while actors and actresses used them as dressing rooms. The joviality is not difficult to imagine — wine flowing, goblets clinking, lanterns ablaze in a background of haunting flute sounds. The entire atmosphere was profligate and the surroundings ornate.

A winding gallery east of the pond is designed to give one the feeling of walking on rippling water.

The pavilions and towers in the Humble Administrator's Garden have been built for recreation, viewing scenery, and decoration. The shapes are most varied in the Zhang Garden Annex — square, round and octagonal. Some structures are set on hills, others on mini-islands in the centre of ponds, but all lend an exotic touch to the garden.

A feeling of natural beauty within the con-fines of a city garden.

Lush trees and vines at
the water's edge add to
the beauty of the garden.

A rocky ravine made by hand.

Halls and pavilions overhang the pond west of the Distant
Fragrance Hall. The Little Flying Rainbow (*Xiao Fei
Hong*) is the name given to this covered bridge.

Golden carp and lotus under the bridge.

Water-lilies.

South of the Little Flying Rainbow is the water courtyard of Miniature Green Wave Pavilion (*Xiao Cang Lang*) where three pavilions overlook water on both sides.

The Lotus-Surrounded Pavilion (*He Feng Si Mian Ting*) occupies a small triangular island. The pavilion is an elegantly ornamented hexagon set amid lotus-beds.

The Hill-Viewing Tower (*Jian Shan Lou*) in the north garden.

Looking north from the Moored Boat (*Han Chuan*) at the north edge of the pond.

Scene from Hill-Viewing Tower, showing the Moored Boat, Little Flying Rainbow and Distant Fragrance Hall in the background.

Willow-shaded galleries wind their way to every point of interest.

Looking west from Another World (*Bie You Dong Tian*) in the central garden.

The Thirty-Six Pairs of Mandarin Ducks Hall (*San Shi Liu Yuan Yang Guan*) is the main building in the west garden. At each corner of the hall, which served its former owner as a banqueting and theatrical hall, is a small square room.

Like walking on waves.

Furniture in the Thirty-Six Pairs of Mandarin Ducks Hall. Fashioned of gnarled boxwood and *nannu* wood and inlaid with marble, the pieces conform to the natural twisting and intercrossing of roots and branches.

Perched on rocks in the pond south of the Thirty-Six Pairs of Mandarin Ducks Hall is the octagonal Pagoda Shaded Pavilion (*Ta Ying Ting*), one of the most exquisite in the garden.

Fan Pavilion (*Shan Ting*) has stone table and stools, and also windows, all fan-shaped.

Potted azalea.

A miniature landscape of bamboo and rock in the extreme west garden, a section devoted to potted plants and miniature landscapes.

The Lingering Garden as depicted by a painter.

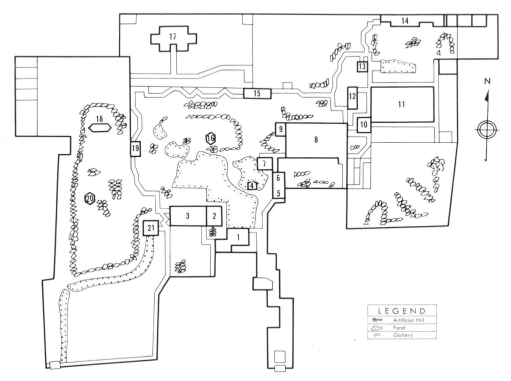

The small flower-adorned court housing the painting of the garden. Located just inside the main gate, it is flanked by halls with galleries.

1 Shaded Walk
2 Bright Zither Tower
3 Green Mountain Cottage
4 Riverside Pavilion
5 Winding Stream Tower
6 West Tower
7 Clear Wind Pond Hall
8 Five-Peak Immortals Hall
9 The Place to Treasure Tradition
10 Bowing Hill Hall
11 Ancient Rustics Lodge
12 Return My Study
13 Pavilion of Welcome Rain and Snow
14 Cloud-Capped Pavilion
15 Distant Green Pavilion
16 Charming Pavilion
17 Another View
18 Pavilion of Utter Delight
19 Cassia Fragrance Hall
20 Calmed Wind Pavilion
21 Lively Place

LEGEND
Artificial Hill
Pond
Gallery

Lingering Garden
(*Liu Yuan*)

The Lingering Garden (*Liu Yuan*) is considered one of the four great gardens of China, the other three being the Humble Administrator's Garden, the Summer Palace in Beijing and the Imperial Mountain Resort at Chengde in Hebei Province. The latter two were imperial gardens in the Qing Dynasty.

With an area of three hectares, the Lingering Garden highlights the ancient Chinese architectural art complemented by hills, water, flowers and trees. It features many exquisitely decorated buildings in compact arrangement. With a maze of doors of different shapes leading to constantly changing scenes, the garden affords the visitor a new vista with nearly every step. This contrasts with the spacious Humble Administrator's Garden with its rustic flavor.

Interesting in the Lingering Garden is its division into distinct landscaped architectural areas connected by more than 700 metres of winding galleries. contoured to the garden's surface, these galleries take one to the water's edge and over the hills. On rainy days one can walk to any of the scenic areas without an umbrella and not get wet. Contrasts are used to perfection between crooked and straight, light and shade, high and low.

A gateway in a low garden wall leads into a curving gallery with a wall inlaid with 300 stone plaques inscribed in cursive or more formal calligraphy depicting the handwriting of masters of past dynasties. A connoisseur of Chinese calligraphic art will understandably spend some time lingering here. The windows are polygons intricately latticed and spaced on the wall between the inscriptions to offer glimpses of fascinating scenes on the other side. At the end of the gallery and beyond a few pavilions is the central section of the garden.

This, and the eastern section, are the two focal points of interest in the garden, though a western section and a northern one are worth visiting as well.

The central section consists mainly of a pond screened by steep rockeries at its northern and western edges, with water between. Shaded by a variety of centuries-old trees, the rocky banks here are indented to suggest having been shaped by the washing of waves. The eastern and southern edges in contrast are built up with towers, galleries and pavilions presenting serried roofs against the natural beauty of the northern and western sections.

By the pond is the Green Mountain Cottage (*Han Bi Shan Fang*) whose wide terraces on the north command a fine view of adjacent scenes and their reflection in the pond. To the south is a courtyard featuring Taihu rockeries and flower-decorated terraces.

Magnificent halls with verandas and zigzag galleries draw the visitor's attention in the eastern part of the Lingering Garden. Outstanding among them are the Five-Peak Immortals Hall (*Wu Feng Xian Guan*) and the Ancient Rustics Lodge (*Lin Quan Qi Shuo Guan*). The beams and pillars of the Five-Peak Immortals Hall are of *nanmu* wood. Its walls and furniture, of the same wood, are carved with inscriptions or landscapes of great masters and other decorative designs. Taihu rockeries in front and galleries and flower-lined paths in back lend elegance to the hall.

Variety is the essence here. Doorways and windows of
many different patterns and designs delight the eye.

A latticed gallery window.

The Ancient Rustics Lodge is partitioned by an immense exquisitely carved screen incorporating two moon-shaped doors. The centre is an immense Chinese painting with calligraphy on the reverse side, both engraved. This screen-partition is a gem of ancient Chinese wood-carving, while the hall and lodge are masterpieces of Chinese landscape garden architecture. With a small richly decorated courtyard in between, the two halls are connected by a winding covered walk. Openings in the wall along the covered walk give visitors one fantastic scene after another on the other side or in the small open spaces between the covered walk and the courtyard wall.

A grove of maples on an earth-and-stone hill in the western section of the Lingering Garden shades two pavilions in spring and summer and floods the landscape in ochre tones in autumn. Below the hill is a small stream, a waterside pavilion known as "Frolic", where the ancient lute was played, and a flower nursery.

The northern section is quite rustic in atmosphere. Grapevines on a long trellis shade the meandering path here. To its south flowering peach, apricot and plum trees fill the spring with their colourful blossoms.

Indispensable to a Chinese garden are miniature landscapes and dwarfed trees in pots and trays, and these are exhibited in the northern section of the Lingering Garden. Their composition is of small rocks, plants, tiny trees and houses, boats, bridges and figurines, the idea being to bring natural scenery in miniature into the room and compensate for lack of green trees and flowering plants in a small space.

Miniature landscape gardening dates back 1,000 years in China. An old centre of this traditional art was the Hill River Bank (*Shantang*) in the suburbs of Suzhou where the art persists, having for centuries been handed down from father to son.

Octagonal doorways in a winding gallery offer different scenes.

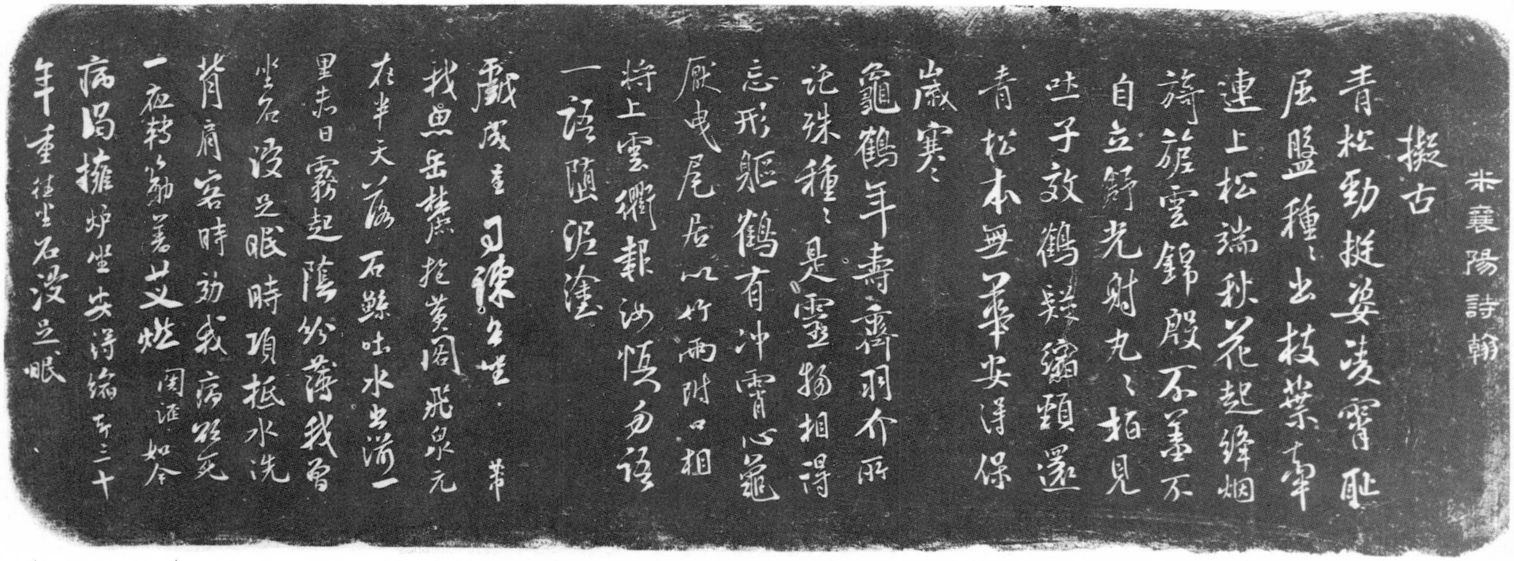

米襄陽詩翰

擬古

青松勁挺姿凌霄恥
屈盤種種出枝葉
連上松端秋花起絳煙
蔣蕤雲錦殷不墨
自立篩光射九九柏見
吐子敦鶴髮繚頸還
青松本無華安得保
歲寒
龜鶴年壽齊羽介兩
詎殊種種是靈揚相得
忘形窺鶴有沖霄心龜
厭曳尾居以竹兩附口相
將上雲衢報沙恨勿語
一語隨泥塗

戲成呈司諫台坐 芾

我魚年蕪抱葉圖飛泉元
在半天矯石駿吐水出滑一
里夫日霧起陰紛薄我曾
坐名沒足眠時頂抵水洗
背肩客時勁我病輕死
一在耘勤著艾燃開誰如今
病喎擁炉坐石沒足眠
年重裡坐石沒足眠

Calligraphy in stone by Mi Fu (1051-1107), one of four master calligraphers of the Song Dynasty. The others were Cai Xiang, Su Dongpo and Huang Tingjian.

Inscription in Huang Tingjian's calligraphy.

庭堅頓首啓

教審
侍奉萬福爲慰承
讀書保嗇深慰間樂其壽
鶴鳴兄寄示十一篇妙曲作樂
尚未就示還俟太爲但寄書大
字頗蒼老行書頗有矮師乃佳
遠荅廣家奉書甚愛塵壹
之坐奉以下

庭堅再拜寓者欲作詩祖
行固循不就今已不作待經年拕
索去而得也字作一扁詔石賦寄上
玆可以爲刻之幸甚
上廣才美諸公必知之
庭堅頓首兩厚
垂顧其真放逐不爲閒廢久事
不能秦詣甚愧未厚之意所
須拙字天涼意或然三俟
閒生枘又取之六十老人五月揮
汗令寒不就辦以於聰明之旺
密以承晚涼遠行于方珍愛
蒙江皆款識舊但藏嘉外遂於事
硯附末就作書

見召乃迢以此爲
庭堅頓首

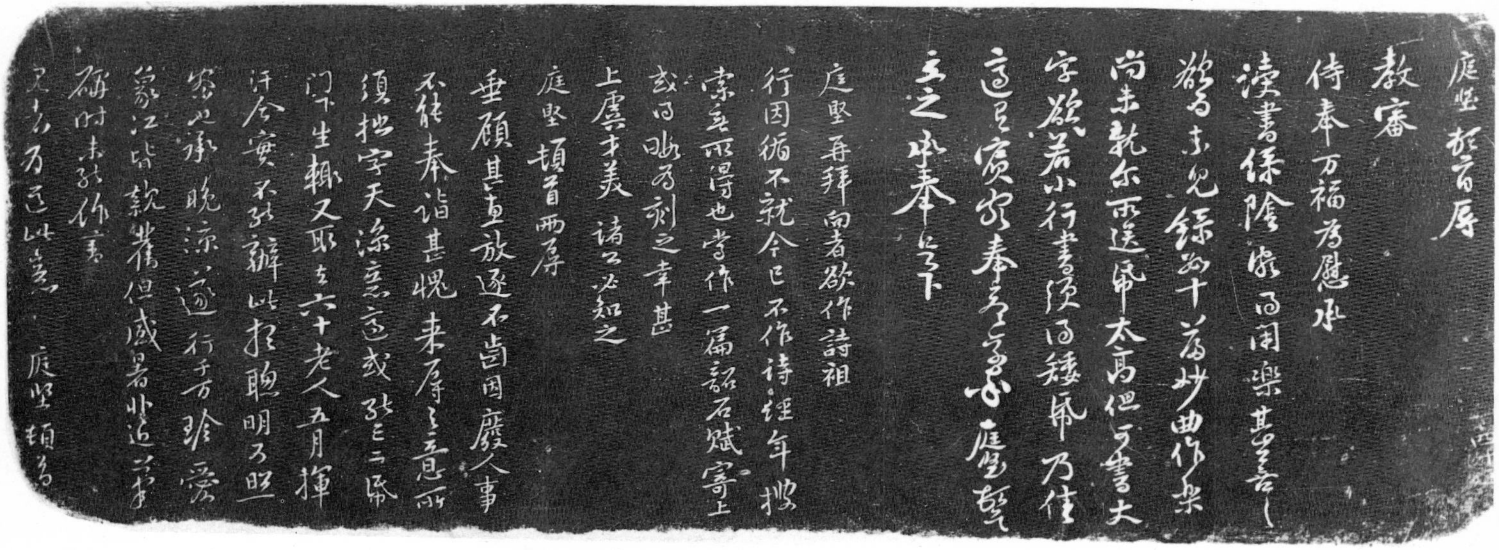

The central section of the Lingering Garden behind a "cloud wall", a basic Suzhou garden structure for marking off scenic areas. The wall is grey-tiled and neatly whitewashed on both sides.

The ground floor of the Bright Zither Tower. The pavilion (*left*) is built on an islet in the pond.

Dominating the garden's central section is a pond surrounded by a hill, trees, halls and pavilions. The Green Mountain Cottage (*Han Bi Shan Fang*) and the Bright Zither Tower (*Ming Se Lou*) stand on its eastern edge.

A crooked bridge canopied with wisteria links the islet with Riverside Pavilion (*Hao Pu Ting*).

Riverside Pavilion.

The eastern and southern edges of the pond.

A stream flows languidly between rockeries north of the pool.

A rocky projection into the pond.

Craggy rocks by the pond.

The *nanmu*-wood-panelled Five-Peak Immortals Hall (*Wu Feng Xian Guan*) in the east garden where the finest architecture is found.

Long casement windows in the hall.

Window lattice.

A floor-to-ceiling openwork screen and latticed window.

A carved hardwood screen-partition incorporating doorways
in the Ancient Rustics Lodge (*Lin Quan Qi Shuo Guan*).

Close-up of one of the doorways, a masterpiece of Chinese carving.

Cloud-Nestling Peak (*Xiu Yun Feng*) on the left.

North of the Ancient Rustics Lodge is the court of the Cloud-Capped Tower (*Guan Yun Lou*). This five-metre high rock, fancifully named Cloud-Capped Peak (*Guan Yun Feng*), gracefully dominates two other lesser "peaks".

Auspicious Cloud Peak (*Rui Yun Feng*) on the right. It is said that these ornamental rocks sank in Taihu Lake by accident when they were being shipped as tribute to the Song Dynasty imperial household. Centuries later they were retrieved and erected here.

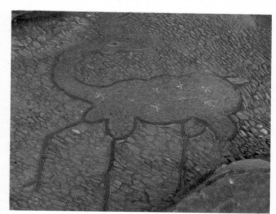

Walkways and courts are often paved in
mosaics of different coloured pebbles.

Walkway and courtyard mosaic patterns.

Potted plants displayed in the north garden.

The shaded pond in the West Garden into which Buddhist monks and devotees placed fish, shrimps and turtles to save them from the cooking pot. The crooked bridges connecting with the Mid-Lake Pavilion (*Hu Xin Ting*) are seen in the foreground and the background.

West Garden
(*Xi Yuan*)

The West Garden (*Xi Yuan*) is unique among Suzhou gardens for its gilded wood sculptures, which offer diversion from the rest.

The West Garden and Lingering Garden, across a roadway, were parts of the private estate of a Ming Dynasty Superintendent Imperial Groom, Xu Shitai, whose son Xu Rong donated the part west of the road to Buddhist monks as the site of a monastery. Hence its name West Garden.

The Heavenly King Hall (*Tian Wang Dian*), the first building inside the front gate, is guarded by two fierce-miened generals in iron armour on each side. Known in Chinese Buddhist lore as the Four Heavenly Kings, or Four Guardians, they were said to ward off danger from the four directions of heaven. In the middle is the pot-bellied Monk Maitreya, with his chest bared, a bag in one hand and a kindly smile playing around the corners of his mouth. This set of clay figures are works of the late Qing Dynasty.

Next is the Buddha Hall (*Da Xiong Bao Dian*) where the central

The Buddha Hall (*Da Xiong Bao Dian*), one of the three main buildings in the garden. The other two are the Heavenly King Hall (*Tian Wang Dian*) and the Arhat Hall (*Luo Han Tang*).

Painted clay sculptures of the four Heavenly Kings, the guardians of a Buddhist monastery.

104

Details of the painted sculptures of the arhats attending Guan Yin, Goddess of Mercy, in the Buddha Hall.

wood sculpture is Buddhism's founder Sakyamuni Buddha, with the Eternal Buddha Amitabha and Vaidurya Buddha, reliever of distress and curer of disease, on his right and left respectively. These are flanked by 10 guardian gods on each side of the hall, 20 in all. The Sakyamuni Buddha, known also as the Buddhist Patriarch, is attended by two disciples, the elder Kasyapa Buddha who first expounded the Patriarch's teachings, and Ananda Buddha, the Most Learned. To the latter is attributed the authorship of the Buddhist Sutras, for he was said to have recorded from memory Sakyamuni's teachings after the master ascended to heaven. The three Buddhas and their two god-general escorts are all superbly executed. One stalwart and handsome figure inclines forward, the balance of the sculpture being maintained by his flowing garment behind. Waves in the base of the statues conceal air holes designed to keep the figures dry and in good condition in the humid climate of south China. All the images display different features and temperaments.

Most interesting and human, perhaps, are the five hundred arhats in forty-eight galleries of the Arhat Hall (*Luo Han Tang*). "Arhat" is the Sanskrit for "one who merits the common people's respect and offerings". Five hundred arhats are mentioned in Chinese Buddhist canons as evidence of the flourishing of the faith, though they were given names only during the Southern Song Dynasty (1127-1279), taken from Buddhist sutras. Buddhas are sculptured conventionally in China, but depiction of arhats allowed relative freedom of the artists' talent and creativeness. The images in the West Garden suggest congeniality, individuality and imagination. Some sit cross-legged in contemplation, others are muscular and pugilistic, battling tigers and dragons. Some are decrepit, with sagging cheeks and chins. Some appear as pedants or scholars, with books in their hands. Monk Ji Gong, the Succourer, is probably the most fascinating, his image conforming in every detail to descriptions in Chinese folklore.

Monk Ji Gong was supposed to have magic powers beneath his crippled and scabby appearance. He would be seen in worn monk's headgear and robe, holding a tattered plantain fan, and likely with a silly grin on his face. He is said to have ridiculed high officials and sympathized with the poor, and was therefore adored by the common people. The image wears a sash so well carved that it appears like silk, while the folds in the wooden garment look real. The monk's facial profile from the left bespeaks tragedy, while from the right it is comic, the mouth turning up on one side and down on the other, though the effect does not seem grotesque. The sculptor has used the Chinese traditional technique of blending realistic delineation with artistic imagination to create a most affable monk image.

A miniature mountain in clay with wood statues of Buddhas forms the centrepiece of the hall whose four sides represent the great sacred mountains of China — Wutai in Shanxi, Emei in Sichuan, Jiuhua in Anhui and Putuo in Zhejiang. Since these mountains were practically inaccessible in olden times, Chinese Buddhists fulfilled their vow to make pilgrimages to them by bowing before the four sides of this clay representation.

Outside the west side-gate of the hall is an open ground with a pond at the centre. Into the sanctuary of this pond Buddhists would place fish and turtles which they had bought to let live as a humanitarian act. A pavilion has been built in the pond with zigzag bridges on either side connecting it with the willow-lined shore. Here, one can sit quietly in the shade or watch the fish nibble at tidbits the visitors throw in.

The Thousand-Armed Guan Yin, carved of camphor-wood on a lotus pedestal, in the Arhat Hall.

The 500 arhats fill 48 galleries in the hall.

A Buddha-mountain in the Arhat Hall. On the four sides are Buddhas representing the four mountains of China which are sacred to Buddhists.

Monk Ji Gong, the Succourer, with his tattered fan. The work shows unconventional genius and strong individuality, traits which are said to have marked the man himself.

Monk Ji Gong grins on one side of his face...

...while grimacing on the other.

In early Qing, professing to stand above politics, the garden's new owner styled himself Wang Shi (Fisherman) and also gave the name to his garden. Shown are two coloured sculptured bricks in the garden.

The carved brick entrance to the Fisherman's Garden. Opening onto a lane, the garden closely links landscaping with architecture, blending both into a harmonious whole.

1   Serenity and Attainment
2   Accumulated Kindness Hall
3   Picking Beauty Tower
4   Serried Cloud Hall
5   Five-Peak Study
6   Accumulated Emptiness Studio
7   Hall for Enjoying Pine and
     Pictures
8   End of Spring Study
9   Cold Spring Pavilion
10 Moon and Breeze Pavilion
11 Ribbon-Washing Hall
12 Cassia Hillock Pavilion
13 Following Harmony Hall
14 Music Room

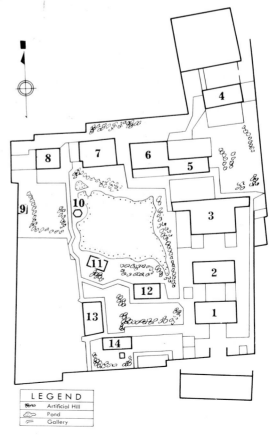

LEGEND

Artificial Hill
Pond
Gallery

The pool that highlights the landscaping of the garden.

Fisherman's Garden (*Wang Shi Yuan*)

Situated in southern Suzhou, the Fisherman's Garden (*Wang Shi Yuan*) is among the city's smallest gardens — only 0.6 hectare. Still it attracts both local and foreign visitors. At times the garden is so crowded that queues form to snap pictures of choice views there, while the flow of people along its paths is like the flow of water in its streams. What makes such a small garden so attractive? Its charm is chiefly man-made — a product of its architects' skill.

The Fisherman's Garden was the residence of an influential Southern Song Dynasty official. During the reign of Emperor Qian Long in the Qing Dynasty, part of the garden was bought by a retired official, Song Zongyuan, who added buildings until they occupied nearly a third of the area. Surprisingly, a cramped feeling is avoided by a wide variation of scenes and skilful execution producing split level effects and a balance between density and sparsity.

The landscaping clearly delineates the garden into three parts. The eastern part was the residential section of its former owner. It had three courtyards, with a sedan-chair "garage", guest room and main hall. Elegantly furnished, it typified the living quarters of feudal scholar-officials.

The western part is no more than a small courtyard set off by itself and decorated in its own style.

Between these units is the garden proper, with water at the centre. Entering from the sedan-chair "garage", one finds oneself in a small square hall named Cassia Hillock Pavilion (*Xiao Shan Cong Gui Xuan*) whose windows look out on four different scenes

Rockeries with cassia trees surround Cassia Hillock Pavilion (*Xiao Shan Cong Gui Xuan*).

An artificial crag framed by an ornamental window.

in the garden. The south window frames an artificial hill of Taihu rocks, and as the name indicates, cassia trees form a cool green grove. Tastefully planted among groupings of Taihu rocks on the other three sides are magnolia, Chinese flowering crabapple, pine and bamboo, presenting live scenes that appear very much like Chinese paintings. West through a gallery is a pool banked with rocks which are perforated in various shapes and from which water oozes. The effect is one of a greater water area than actually exists, and also of fluidity. Galleries, pavilions, halls and studios are built beside this main pool as well and are complemented with plants of the four seasons. The pool contains no plants but appears as a mirror reflecting the sky, hills, pavilions, halls and trees. This use of water to mirror scenes is another device to multiply levels and enrich the scene. Practically every step the visitor takes here is rewarded with a different and delightful scene.

The Chinese garden exhibited in New York's Metropolitan Museum of Art was designed on the model of the End of Spring Study (*Dian Chun Yi*). This garden is situated in the northwest corner of the Fisherman's Garden. Built during the Ming Dynasty, it is an exquisite representative of that style, including the carved hardwood furnishings and palace lanterns. Referred to as Ming Style Hall (*Ming Xuan*), its proper name originates from the blooming in late spring of peonies planted there.

Behind the buildings in the garden of the End of Spring Study are bamboo clusters, plantain trees and an overlooking artificial hill. Pebbles now pave the front yard; the peonies have been restored. A stone stairway at the southwest corner leads down to a pool alongside which is a stone tablet inscribed Clear Water Spring (*Han Bi Quan*). This spring together with the tablet were discovered in 1958 when the yard was being rebuilt.

Its eastern bank.

The western bank of the pool.

The Moon and Breeze Pavilion (*Yue Dao Feng Lai Ting*) at the pool's eastern edge.

Here, blue water reflects quiet scenes.

Two steps and you're across this tiny arched stone bridge.

A curving bridge.

Scene through a latticed window.

Ancient pine and cypress at the northern edge of the pool with the Ribbon-Washing Hall (*Zhuo Ying Shui Ge*) in the background.

Latticed full-length casements in the Hall for Enjoying Pine and Pictures (*Kan Song Du Hua Xuan*) at the pool's northern edge.

Among the old paintings preserved in the hall is this *Land of Peach Blossoms* by Zhou Chen, a Ming Dynasty painter born in Suzhou and known especially for his landscape paintings.

Viewing Apricot Blossom by the celebrated Ming Dynasty painter Tang Yin (1470-1523), also born in Suzhou and known for his paintings of landscapes, figures, flowers and birds, calligraphy and poems.

The carved hardwood casements in the hall.

The Serried Cloud Hall (*Ti Yun Shi*). The interior is lavishly decorated with intricately carved hardwood filigree.

Water-carved rocks viewed through
long casements in the hall.

Carved panels in the casements.

129

Carvings in the lower part of the casements include buildings and landscapes.

A zigzag gallery lined with rockeries, flowering plants and shrubs.

The End of Spring Study (*Dian Chun Yi*) in Ming Dynasty architectural style, a small secluded area in the northwest garden. It is so named because peonies that used to bloom here "said goodbye to spring".

Bamboo and rock through a carved window frame.

A graceful plantain at the window.

1   Jade Pavilion
2   Carefree in All Four Seasons
    Pavilion
3   Bowing Stone Pavilion
4   Music Hall of the Hillside
    Immortal
5   Stone Terrance
6   Green-Clad Pavilion
7   Golden Grain Pavilion

8   Small Green Wave Pavilion
9   Chignon Pavilion
10 Gallery Hall
11 Crystal Dew Hall
12 Wall-Facing Pavilion
13 Phoenix Perching in a Parasol
     Tree
14 Lotus-Root Fragrance Pavilion
15 South Snow Pavilion

The relatively small Garden of Ease is divided into east and west parts by a partitioned gallery.

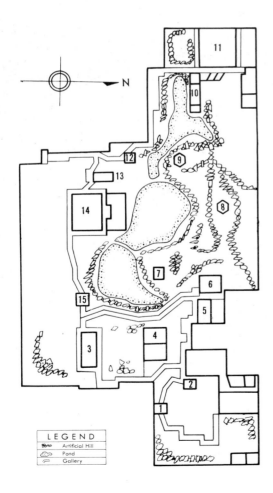

LEGEND
Artificial Hill
Pond
Gallery

Garden of Ease
(*Yi Yuan*)

Built approximately in 1875 in the late Qing Dynasty, this garden was formerly a private estate of the Qing official Gu Wenbin. It is said to have taken seven years to build and cost 200,000 taels of silver.

It is the newest of Suzhou's gardens. A mere century old, the Garden of Ease (*Yi Yuan*) incorporates strong points of other gardens. It is compact, and displays rich variation in landscape. The best Taihu rocks were salvaged from the ruins of three other gardens to lend their unique beauty to this late-comer among Suzhou gardens.

The garden occupies little more than a half hectare, a partitioned gallery with latticed windows on the central wall dividing this into eastern and western parts. Strolling along the gallery one can enjoy these latticed windows and the scenes they frame, some from the western part of the garden. Intriguing also is the fact that visitors on either side of the central wall of the partitioned gallery can see and talk to each other while being quite beyond each other's reach. It is patterned after the partitioned gallery at the water's edge at the Green Wave Pavilion. This gallery has at its northern extremity the Greenery-Clad Pavilion (*Suo Lu Xuan*), while the South Snow Pavilion (*Nan Xue Ting*) lies to its south. Gates at either end lead west.

The eastern part of the garden features mainly courtyards and garden structures landscaped with flowering plants, trees and rockeries and surrounded by winding galleries. Their picture-windows are outstanding for the scenes they frame.

Hills and water are the main components of the western part, the main scenic spot of the garden. As in the Fisherman's Garden, a pool of water forms the garden's centre. Wide in the middle, the pool appears to have an east and west wing, the eastern one being spanned by a crooked bridge, while the western one features a series of "water gates" and bends formed of Taihu rocks. The effect is one of neither beginning nor end of water. Artificial hills and rockeries occupy the area north of the pool. They are low and exhibit peaks, caverns and valleys with trees and pavilions above which appear as real hills. Of all of Suzhou gardens the Garden of Ease probably has the most artistically arranged artificial hills, with access from both the east and the west. A cavern on the western side has a stalactite hanging from its roof; below are a stone table and stone stools. A passageway leads into momentary loss of bearings, but wriggling through brings the venturesome out again into the brightness of a small open space. Make your way up another hill and you cross a bridge to the hill top. Here the entire garden comes into full view. The Chignon Pavilion (*Luo Ji Ting*), dainty and exquisite with eaves within one's reach, is a good match for the small hill. There is no getting down the hill other than by its labyrinth of paths.

The Lotus-Root Fragrance Pavilion (*Ou Xiang Xian*) south of the pool is surrounded by a veranda and divided inside into the south and north halls by long windows. Behind the pavilion is a terrace by the pool, while to its south a small courtyard displays a serried flower bed studded with rockeries and planted to peonies of both the ordinary and tree varieties, osmanthus and lace-bark pines.

The atmosphere west of the Lotus-Root Fragrance Pavilion with its diminutive courtyards and jutting trees is one of ancient stillness and serenity. Further west is a pleasure boat modelled after the Moored Boat in the Humble Administrator's Garden, from which swimming fish can be viewed, while behind the "boat" is a decorative stone wall around which are planted bamboo and other trees. A gallery east of the Lotus-Root Fragrance Pavilion connects it with the South Snow Pavilion.

The Lotus-Root Fragrance Pavilion (*Ou Xiang Xuan*), the main building in the west garden, where water is the keynote. The terrace is known as a place for viewing the scenery and fish.

A "water gate" in the east pool.

Carvings on wood in the pavilion of paintings by the celebrated Qing Dynasty painter Zheng Banqiao (1693-1756), with inscriptions in his own calligraphy. Zheng Banqiao, a native of Jiangsu Province, excelled in depicting bamboo, rockeries and orchids in strong, staccato strokes.

138

The rockery as seen
from the Lotus-Root
Fragrance Pavilion.

The Golden Millet Pavilion (*Jin Su Ting*).

The Carefree in All Four Seasons Pavilion (*Si Shi Xiao Sha Ting*) courtyard with its winding gallery in the east garden.

DATE DUE